The Pollination Field

The Pollination Field

Poems

Kim Fahner

TURNSTONE PRESS

The Pollination Field

Turnstone Press
Artspace Building
206-100 Arthur Street
Winnipeg, MB
R3B 1H3 Canada
www.TurnstonePress.com

Turnstone Press gratefully acknowledges the assistance of the Canada Council for the Arts, the Manitoba Arts Council, the Government of Canada through the Canada Book Fund, and the Province of Manitoba through the Book Publishing Tax Credit and the Book Publisher Marketing Assistance Program.

Printed and bound in Canada by Friesens.

Library and Archives Canada Cataloguing in Publication

Title: The pollination field : poems / Kim Fahner.
Names: Fahner, Kim, 1970- author
Identifiers: Canadiana (print) 20250115611 | Canadiana (ebook) 2025011562X | ISBN 9780888017987 (softcover) | ISBN 9780888017994 (EPUB) | ISBN 9780888018007 (PDF)
Subjects: LCGFT: Poetry.
Classification: LCC PS8561.A3784 P65 2025 | DDC C811/.54—dc23

MANITOBA ARTS COUNCIL
CONSEIL DES ARTS DU MANITOBA

Canada Council for the Arts
Conseil des arts du Canada

Funded by the Government of Canada
Financé par le gouvernement du Canada
Canada

Manitoba

For the bees, and all of the other pollinators,
and for the wise women of Ireland,
and for Terry …

Contents

Second Tale: Queen Bee, Mother of All

The Pollination Field

Telling the Bees

Cortege

Third Tale: Coda—A Bee Reflection

The Pollination Field

A Bee in the House

Deep July and it buzzes, like a simple housefly,
but then with a baritone that conjures a bagpipe's drone
as it gets closer to panic—not able to find its way home.

A day of hours later, silenced, it falls to the hardwood floor,
curled into itself like a strange semi-colon—a pause—
punctuated by stillness, antennae shivering in a breeze.

Hold it in the palm of your hand,
let it roll from side to side. It might
tell your fortune if you're lucky.

Stained glass, those wings, like tiny windows
you look through, trying to find answers to questions
that have only been imagined, never asked.

A bird in the house means death, but a bee is good luck.
So how do the two creatures meet? Around corners, unseen—in quiet,
premeditated affairs, hidden messages, or broadcast in bold bunting,

hashtags that are hung out to say, skankily,

'X' marks the spot

&

this is mine, not yours.

First Tale:
The Queen in the Bee-Loud Glade

Preface: Origin

Seal the envelope with a circle of melted wax, colour of blood and imprinted with crest of sharp hexagonal cell and crisp angle carved in the stylized likeness of a bee's wing. Message in a bottle, a letter passed through time—not through post office or red mailbox—to be opened by this storied and legendary one, an oracle who minds her charges.

She breaks the wax seal, reads the tale: first, there is the beekeeper, all-Tilley-hat-clad, and then the one who is out in the woods, so beloved of the bees.

There is more than one queen: a string of them, one transforming into another, swirls of sequinned, gossamer gowns that spiral out as they dance—one queen dying, and then the other one arriving.

But, before all that, this is how it begins.

i) In the Beginning

When did the bees arrive, and who wrote their story? When did the winged things come down from the sky, descending from another dimension? Were the fireflies their ancestrals, their oracles, their ancient wise women who looked into reflective pools to scry the future?

Were they here before the creatures that existed long, long before the story of a biblical ark was inked onto woven strips of Nile papyrus? When there were strange dinosaurs with wings and painted tails, wild dragons with sharpest teeth and reptilian eyes?

Maybe they were here before the early humans who left their footprints embedded in African soil. Then, Lucy strode—*Australopithecus!*—proof that we began to walk upright at a fixed point in time. There was, too, a time when the dinosaurs disappeared: *End-Cretaceous.* Beyond that, there were a few times when glaciers slid back and forth across continents with the ease of a lover's hand sweeping along the curve of a waist, or across and down the slope of strong shoulders.

The earth gives up its evidence—in ambered pieces, in fossils, in archaeological and geological digs. What's written on papyrus may or may not be true. Who is to say?

Here, in Northern Ontario, there were mists, geological fault lines moaning and sighing as they mated roughly, splitting nickel from copper long before there were mine shafts sunk into deepest depths of earth by human hands.

And so, when did the bees arrive?

ii) Once Upon a Time …

… there was a woman who lived deep in the woods, tended to only by squirrels, bluebirds, and fireflies that draped her in woven ribbons of light. Stand far away from her and she would chameleon herself into the bush, sinking backwards into the grey of a rocky ledge overlooking the lake, or else sitting cross-legged on a patch of lichen, all blue-green and wet with dew and longing. From afar, she looked like a statue, carved into (and out of) the earth and air. Elemental. From afar, she melded into geology and ecology, drawing ferns around her hips and boughs of cedar across her breasts. She was rooted.

At dawn, she cast off her ferns, her cedar boughs, raised her arms like branches to the sky—wide open and naked.

They came then, the bees.

In town, people felt them before they saw them—a vibration, a ripple in the air.

It shifted, the air, and the light was darkened by thousands of tiny wings beating all at once. Down the main street, around the cul-de-sacs, the bees gathered, mustering themselves into squadrons—workers and drones. Called to her by something prehistoric. People felt it, shut their windows, closed storm doors, thought twice about leaving their dogs outside, and wished the sparrows well. People shivered.

The bees had arrived.

She felt it in her core, their coming and then their arrival. Sensed their spinning at her root, in her gut, in the bird cage of her chest, and in the centre of her forehead—third eye—the place where dreams were spun, conjured like wax honeycomb.

From under the pale skin of her bare feet, from under the mossy patch where she stood, the ground hummed, prescient. There was no fear. They had arrived, the bees. They rejoiced. They sang.

The queen has been found.

iii) The Greeting

The air shimmered, the earth shivered, the lake swirled up into being, and the sun turned to look away. They descended into the woods, those bees, carpeted the grove of cedars and firs, hovering in the branches of birches, clustering in the abandoned nests of spring's fallen robins. They peered over edges of twigs and the rough shingles of pinecones. They hitched rides on the backs of dragonflies that hovered in mid-air, all magic.

She stood, statue. Could not even take a breath in or out. Was sculpted, frozen, captured.

The bees waited.

    She waited.

They waited.

    She waited.

They took a breath in, all together, then let it out in unison. A sighing, a letting go. They had arrived, after such a long journey.

* * *

She felt her fingers twitch, tiny flicks of internal electrics on fire. Expectant, full of desire. She turned her palm upwards, open, beckoned them nearer. One bobbled bee rose from a bit of wild yellow yarrow—wobbled, hummed, buzzed.

It rose slowly, bumbled and burdened by the weight of its body. Moved to the edge of her index finger. Landed.

Welcome.

iv) The Fashioning

She stood naked in the centre of the grove, pines circling. Her skin, pale ivory, soon shapeshifted into something other. They came, laced themselves gently in living garlands around her neck, breasts, torso—dressed her in a gold Egyptian collar of moving wings, humming their accompaniment to her heartbeat.

She both knew and did not know that she was the queen of this new colony.

They began to dress her slowly with the furry curves
    of their rounded bellies, small mouths, flickering antennae.

At first, a soft frisson of energy, a ripple that ran from the soles of her feet
    up to the very top of her skull.

Then, a quiet kissing, tiny wings creating sound and bee bodies
    swarming in symphonic unison.

They fed her wax and honey as her eyes were slowly woven shut,
    fastened together by the gifts of bees' kisses.

She could breathe, but barely.
    She stood, statue.

She waited.

The bees waited.

She waited.

They waited.

A silence descended upon the grove:
wings stilled, wind shushed itself,
and the new queen stood sentinel.

v) A Lesson from the Bees

Inside her waxen cocoon, she felt rather than watched the world go by. At first, the bees seemed only to kiss her skin—tiny licks like lightning through a too-humid sky, shocks of electricity shivering up and down her arms, legs, torso, groin. Electrified.

Their hum increased in intensity, mounting from almost silent to a symphony of vibration that soared to fierce climax. She wept, tears falling in the space between face and wax veil. Spaces between are where the loss lives, where grief resides. Where breaths are taken.

From the inside, she watched slowly as her vision dimmed. At first, only a blur of dampened images, and then milky white, followed by an instant called totality—a solar eclipse badly viewed.

With time, she came to hear the bees, to even understand their words.

They danced their dance, shaking their torsos, caught up in fashioning their home. She was a queen, but not *just a queen*. Here was the queen *and* the hive.

She wondered—

Can one be both?

They thrummed out a synchronized choral response—a pavane across the mossy floor of the glade.

> *Yes. Queen bee and home. Lighthouse and lighthouse keeper all at once. Lock and key together, not apart. Why not both? No separation.*

They answered her, then kept at their work, building layer after layer, covering her in holy veils, encasing her in waxen armour, all while the townspeople hovered on the edge of the glade, watching—from between the pines and birches—confused by her transformation.

***

Her mouth was bound shut, voice shuttered up like a fishing village before a fierce east coast storm. The bees sang to her, songs of sorrow and songs of healing. She listened.

Arias of evolution woven through memory. They told her stories, promised her a new world afterwards. She listened still.

Transformation takes time. Don't rush it.
Silence comes to sit with you first.

vi) Camouflage

Seven days of bee makers making, and then the honeycomb was complete—melding itself to her curves with sensual style. So glorious. Her eyes faded from Atlantic Ocean depths to brushed nickel. Her eyes saw, but also did not see. Her eyes were newly made now, covered in thick lenses of honey and wax, so that she could feel the air shift slightly against the place where her eyelashes used to be.

She could not see.

Nothing was clear.

vii) Beekeeper

The people recruited a beekeeper from out of town, someone who had never seen anything as rare or terrifying as this. Upon arrival in the grove, he walked towards what looked like the wax statue of a woman. Everyone else stood back, agog and afeared.

Whispers ensued:

> *Is that? But … how could it be? What has become of her? How has she changed, transformed?*
>
> *… whoever would have thought …*

And then …

> *… do you think she can be saved? Is it too late? Can we cut her out with pinking shears?*

The beekeeper ignored them all, put on his beige Tilley hat, walked gingerly across the mossiest and rockiest parts of the grove in the black, rocky canyon. Wondered what would happen next. Dispatching smoke from his beekeeping kit, he moved his arms as if he were a dancer rather than a keeper.

He waited.

The bees waited.

He waited.

They waited.

Soon enough, the bees shifted, hovered from there to here, and back again. Someone thought to play a quiet tin whistle, wondering if perhaps music would help the bees move away from the woman inside the honeycomb sarcophagus. From that whistle came a lilting tune by a long-dead composer who had travelled the hills in a different place, another time.

The beekeeper took out a knife, looked for a place where he could begin, could try to open the casing of the over-seven-day-old honeycomb. Moved around the statue of the woman, slowly discerning—as best as possible—whether she lived. Chose the tip of her right index finger. A place to start. Worked away at it and opened a small hole, a portal. It had begun.

She would begin to emerge from the inside out.

viii) Unveiling

The beekeeper borrowed a spare townsperson to help him puff out the smoke—in clouds and mists—around the woman's form. No one could be sure she was still in there. Who knew what might have happened? She might have shrivelled up, as all wise women do when they are wrongly encapsulated by either magic spell or beeswax. She might have vanished, pulled into an invisible vortex, the honeycomb more piñata than something substantial.

He moved closer then, began to poke at the hole in the wax around her index finger. He worked away, persistent at wearing her down. Peeling, peeling, peeling, layer by layer. Somewhere in there, there was a person, a woman who needed to be released. Trapped by silencing that she hadn't requested. Trapped by circumstances that were beyond her control. Now. What to do? What to do?

The beekeeper leaned in close to where the woman's face might be, placed a listening ear up to the spot where her mouth ought to be. Listened. Was that a breath? A whisper? Leaned in again, and then leaned back. Nodded.

The beekeeper leaned in—carefully now!—and made a tiny hole near the corner of her mouth. He picked away at it—carefully, carefully!—and soon enough her lips were revealed. Peeled back layers of thick wax, decimated the hexagons. He moved upwards then, removing wax from around her nose. Put a hand up to her face—so carefully!—to see if she had been able to breathe yet. No? Yes? Maybe … even just the suggestion of a breath?

He listened carefully, took a chance, put his mouth near to hers and breathed breath into her. Hoped for her resurrection. For a moment, nothing.

Then, a gasp.

Breath in.

Breath out.

The queen was awake.

ix) Resurrection and Departure

Some will have written down that resurrection is only ever biblical, that it only has to do with a Christ-like figure, all allegory. But could it not also be about something to do with a witch, an oracle, or wise woman? A tale told by, or about, a woman rather than a man? She is someone who has just shed her skin, been born again. She has cast off the wax gown the bees made her, felt a pine breeze brush against the softest skin of her inner arms and wrists, even her armpits.

What then? What if this one has transformed herself from the past into a present that sings more of the future than of history? Will they shrink back in their seats, the townspeople, if they know she has been brought back to life, after having been encased in wax? Will they gasp at her reanimation, her reincarnation? What will they ask each other?

Where has she been? Who has she been with while she was away? Is she altered forever, or just for a week or so? Shall we bring her wild blueberries from the hill, and sweet mead, to comfort her and offer solace for what's been lost? Has she crossed over? Into some other dimension? Or, has she just become more of herself after all is said and done?

The bees gather round, speaking to her alone:

> *Will you remember what we shared with you?*

She nods, this secret keeper kind of queen bee, not sharing.

* * *

On the day of their departure, en masse, the bees gathered in a circle around the place where their queen used to stand. She has gone now, left them bereft and circling rotten logs in the bush to find a new home. All they are left with is her discarded waxen sheath, someone that they used to know. Proof that she once lived here, too. So lovely. She will not be forgotten but remembered in wing-song forever.

As for you, Dragonfly . . .

The Shape of Supplication

You took the breath from me. It sounds like something my Irish grandmother might have said, once upon a time. *You took the breath from me* and then you brought me to my knees, bent in prayer, in the shape of what a woman looks like at the feet of a man when she is either in love, in lust, or broken. Her mouth, in the shape of an O, either whispered, shouted, or weeping. I gathered you in, but *you still took the breath from me*, like a punch to the gut or solar plexus—whichever is closer, or easiest.

> Viral loads and shedding. Lungs like Chinese sky lanterns that flicker luminaria now. Single flame, tealight, shimmering fire as they rise—caught on breath of wind, unbroken, carried far, far, far up. To where? To top of the sky, into atmosphere, and beyond, to the moon or Mars or maybe just your Saturn Return—annotated
> for future reference and stuffed into the hall closet for safe keeping.

This is the shape of supplication, how I am brought to my knees—bent down before you—my mind a whirl or a wheel or a will-o'-the-wisp. *You took the breath from me, bent me down to the ground, raised my head up while you looked down.* Mary Magdalene had an easier time, kneeling on sand instead of hardwood, saying rosaries around her trauma, lighting luminaria and sending wishes up to the stars.

Trying to catch her breath, not sure if she could.

When the Bees Fly Out of Your Mouth

When that happens, when the words fly
like a swarm of bees from your mouth,
I will bobble my head as if there is water
burbling somewhere in my inner ear—
aquariumed up and packed full of tiny jellyfish
that sting, or sharks that circle, closing in.

Stand on one foot, shake the other leg floppy in mid-air;
watch pathetic fallacy try to get out of the pool by
finding the shallow end after having been out too far,
over my head. But I will stumble and fall,
so unable to get up. Woman down.

Six weeks later and I'll still remember it,
recall the bees throwing themselves suicidal
out of your mouth and onto my living room floor,
so that their wings were crushed in the chaos,
so that mismatched dragonflies in the garden peered
in through the front window and then rolled their bug eyes
back in their insect heads and turned away quickly,
as if to avoid the high drama, the gaslighter conducting
an orchestra without a proper string section.

Inside Out

I am on the inside of a claustrophobic snow globe now,
without give. You are out there, a car parked at the curb,
idling when you ought not to be, hovering and peering in.

In and out, and then gone. Turn a sock inside out, find
the seams that gather things together when nothing else
will contain the brokenness of stories, nails, toes, hearts.

Outside, brick walls and fences that make good neighbours.
In the yard, two trees: the crab apple tree will wed itself
in spring. The mountain ash will try to catch up,

countering with a cluster of red berries, feeding crows in September.
Never one to give up easily, the other will drop ripe apples through the air,
tempting stray starlings and runaway squirrels that highwire acrobatic.

But I am on the inside of this snow globe now, my hands
pressed up against glass—palms open and empty—a mime,
wondering if you'll come again. Knowing you won't.

Code

The splinter in my foot is fashioned from glass, broken sharply off
something that has fallen and shattered on the kitchen floor.
A glass, or a world. It wedges itself into the bottom of my sole.

The sun outside splits the front yard into a nautical marine signal flag.
The sky plays tricks on my eyes, and the lawn signals my thoughts
in code, only to be deciphered—much later—by dandelions in early May.

I chant the code, jot down the words on scrap paper:

Yankee Tango Oscar Delta Echo Golf Juliett Tango Golf India Golf Kilo Mike

I drag an anchor
Keep clear
Man overboard
I maneuver with difficulty
I alter my course to starboard
I require a pilot
I am on fire with dangerous cargo
Keep clear
I require a pilot
I shift my course to port
I require a pilot
I wish to communicate with you
My vessel is stopped

I sit on the floor, extract tiny, slivered bits of glass, watch the blood
river itself into a map of the arch, the ball, the open palm of my foot.

Routine

As you lock doors before bed,
be sure the keys haven't been left outside in
case someone steals them—when they just
dangle there. They might speed off with your car.
Emergencies happen all the time, and bird
feathers drop from the sky, half wings on pavement,
gore on the sidewalk, and who knows how that even
happened. What predator swooped down, fierce,
ignited by a sharp hunger or sense of rough, unbridled
jealousy? Don't ask. The birds will take care of themselves,
killing what's underneath them in the food chain,
loving what's left and guarding the in-between things.
Make sure you turn on the porch light, so that darkness
never seeps onto the front steps, in case intruders try to
open your window, door, life. Next morning, be sure to prepare.
Pack a lunch with a too-tiny juice box, granola bar, piece of fruit.
Question your knowledge of the Canada Food Guide. (Is it still valid?)
Remember to grab a book for your bag, in case of delays or upsets.
Sit carefully with your back up against a wall or a tall tree.
Try to take a deep breath. Pretend you can guide your own meditation.
Use the Force. Channel Yoda, or maybe Pema Chödrön instead.
Vary your word choice, spoken and written. Watch your sentence structure.
Wash your hands carefully, using soap and avoiding hand sanitizer.
Xylophone yourself through the day, one note after another, a bit manic.
Yawn once in a while to clear your ears, mind, heart. Be grateful for oxygen.
Zigzag in mid-afternoon, avoiding moving targets, and humming Bach
to distract.

Grief

The crab apple did not flower in May's humid damp,
pulled itself in after a harsh winter, protested
loudly. Decided not to take part in spring.

Covid Inventory

Take an inventory of lost things:
the smell of garlic browning in a pan,
a friend who vanishes into a pandemic bubble,
a backyard fire pit full of new snow,
the taste of citrus on my tongue.

Surrender

to the uncertainty of the times,
and the sharp bite of January's wind,
along with the wobbly heart, held
in carefully cupped palms, with hope
hitchhiking a ride on a northern highway.

In Your Bones

Water that is cold, but without ice.
A shiver that passes from
head to toe. A manual return on
an antique typewriter, with a bell
that rings. Or a door slam
that sets a gust rushing
through the house.

Tiny Things

Like fruit flies in beakers,
and broken hearts, and mushrooms
that spring up where you least
expect them on wooded hikes,
and the absence of a voice
that was once so dear.

Man, Sleeping on the Living Room Floor

He was an unruly sideshow ghost,
lying on his back, stretched out elastic,
eyes closed, hands at rest by sides, palms open.
Watercolour memory: he's now the blurred
shape of a man, once gentle and kind, worn down.
End of day, my home a nest; lost bird's refuge.
How an unlocked door did not equal
honest mind, open heart, sanctuary's trust.
Feathers bent now, wings frayed by weather;
I close my eyes, see you there, once beloved.

Bee at Sheringham Point Lighthouse

Shirley, British Columbia

Before the handsome man parks his car on the side of Highway 14, strips to his sculpted waist at Jordan River—dog leash in one hand and towel in the other, balancing precariously on pebbled, storm-spent rocks—there is the lighthouse. After the lighthouse, there is the man, the dog that is on and then off a leash, and a keen longing for the strong physicality of a man sculpted, naked. Wide shoulders. Strong arms.

The lighthouse comes before the man on the beach. White against blue of the Strait of Juan de Fuca. White against the bruised blues and blacks and greys of the mountains that rise in Washington State. The lighthouse promises pods of orcas, possibility of humpbacks shifting waves, blowholes firing tsunami warnings, eagles that might flicker in peripheral vision—either eagles, or detached retina.

After the lighthouse comes the highway to Port Renfrew, curled and sinuous—a finger tracing out the makings of a word on your back after sex. Dyslexia stops you from reading the letters, the alphabet disappears as you mix up 't' with 'k,' wondering what he's trying to tell you in silence. Before the man comes the revelation: pebbles on the beach aren't even, sturdy, or steadfast; they shift with the tide, seaweed, shipwrecked hermit crabs.

Before the man, though, there are blackberries. At the trailhead leading down to Sheringham's light. Stop there. Let your finger trace tiny globes hung ornament, green and red. One bloom, and one bee that lingers near it. Don't jump or run. Playing runner and chaser forecasts ruins—of paths, sea roads, outbound tides, abandoned whorls of shell in tidal pools. Stand still. Don't fidget. Say hello and thank the bee for its bounty. Let it hover, buzzing.

Remember this: the lighthouse comes before the man.
The man is not the lighthouse, even if he shines so brightly.

Distinctions are important now.

On the edge of the Strait of Juan de Fuca, Sheringham's light saved men.
Not the other way round. Mind the edge now. The cliffs are steep here.
The signs tell you so. Step badly, slide down to water, miss the bee entirely.

And the bee is still there

        suspended in air

            waiting

        near the blackberry bush.

Winter at Peggy's Cove, Nova Scotia

Your ghost gave me remnants of a hive to take
down to the shore, wax worn down and peeling.

> Peeling, dead skin and proof of life, wax
> fashioned hexagon, memory box cells.

Memory is a cell with a closed door, fashioned lock
without a key. You whisper *return to sea*,

> make me think of returns, keys, an old box
> full of old birth certificates, driver's licences.

We are full of paper, no birth without license to change
until the seals come ashore at the cove, mermaids

> in their wake, ashore, followed by more seals and lobster boats.
> Put the hive down. Rest it on black rocks; don't slip.

Slip and fall, perish. The hive's down, returned to saltwater.
Weep and baptize with saltwater tears. Slip and fall. Don't perish.

Stings

The bee sting happens quickly, a blow off ocean—
warning her what's brewing, stormy cloud formation.

Her storm clouds are dragons—fierce in formation;
a sting to cheek is swollen tongue, speech stuck in throat.

Her speech stops, stung cheek a red balloon, swollen tongue.
Just before it lanced—a quick strike in and out—

she reached out to touch a petal, just before,
took territory that wasn't hers to claim.

Claimed territory that belonged to another: stung.
The bee stung. Her hand slapped frantic, panicked.

Panicked, the bee was sent spinning, dashed to earth.
Spinning head, she bent to earth, watched the bee panic.

Afterwards, panicked, cheek swollen, she bent to earth,
sang the bee a song, offered it—blown kiss—to ocean.

Swim at Own Risk

(after Carolyn Forché)

She knows she cannot swim out to where whales live, cannot fathom
        deepest parts of the sea,
places where whales move like underwater submarines—
        only shifting

when dolphins nudge past in a hurry, rushing to get beyond this strait,
        to open water.
Sea washes the sand in a frill of salt and a *yes* sound.
        Her groin skips a beat, twitches

hopeful, groans with weight of need, desire, longing. These things
        are clear nail polish applied
to the run in her nylons, socks with holes
        where the toes asked for a divorce,

a can opener that only chews into part of the lid, frustrates,
        needs a sharp knife to open.
Her groin skips a beat, half-shell of clam meeting other half—
        staccato conversation in dark.

Morse code, her fingers tap-tap-tapping on her knees;
        she's taking dictation from her body,
not her brain. Stands at edge of sea, where broken hermit crabs
        freeze in *memento mori,*

shaded sepia inside, but orange shell outside—
    as if they're about to haul ass and scuttle
on along the shore. Takes off her suit, doesn't look back.
    Leaves the lycra to the seals.

Itinerary

(after Roo Borson)

As for you, Dragonfly, you leave the island
in the middle of the night, go out
in search of a destination, last junction on a railway line,
terminus point, hotel check-in,

but your wingspan is too broad for landing, four iridescent sails
moved by muscles—
independent and somehow still symphonic.
Hover here, jut there, helicopter

from edge of serrated leaf towards potential prey,
smaller but protein-laden.
You only hunt while flying—for food or mate.
Stopping means starvation.

As for you, a 3 a.m. departure means navigating by moon,
searching for a far shoreline
with faith. Follow: current of air above lake water,
ribbon of wave-ripple.

Or lead, instead. Be the maritime lighthouse, on
an imagined sixth Great Lake, not a lost sailor;
the compass rose or the shifting weathervane; the blood
that rushes through heart, head.

But what of a navigator? Is one needed? Old paper map,
        accordion-pleated, blue highlighted
highways that become country roads called Zion Line in Renfrew.
        Pin that. Amber it in memory.

As the crow flies, it's only a day's drive—from north to southeast.
        On dragonfly wings—
gossamer—a week. By bee, two weeks with fine weather,
        or six months by map, lost.

Mark calendar days with a pen, blood red. Note time
        with three hands of a clock,
one for hour, two for minute, three for quick sweep of seconds
        rushing by river.

Fasten your seatbelt, Dragonfly; review emergency instructions
        in the seat pocket.
Prepare for rough landing. Transformation
        is instinctual, illogical—

Second Tale:
Queen Bee, Mother of All

i) End Stage: Active Dying

The news on the street is that the old queen is failing, so hold onto your hats: the decline is followed by the rising. The word out there, in the hive-hood, is that she can't thrum anymore—her trip-the-light-fandango has gone the way of the dodo bird. She's on her way out.

Shush, now.
        Don't spread rumours.

She may have fallen arches and crow's feet at the corners of her eyes, but don't offer her royal jelly as a cure-all for aging, and don't tell her that it'll mend the low libido.

Shush, now.
        Just be kind.

Turn away.
        Pretend you don't see her.

She's over the hill, over the hive.
    Over.
        Over.
            Over.

ii) Beginnings

This one began as she had done, new and virginal—just as all others before her. She was born, raised on royal jelly served in a silver spoon. Larva into a pupa in just eight days. Take a photo, someone, please! She won't be this new for long, and she may not last the month!

Workers seal her in with wax, this queen bee-to-be. Fifteen days pass like pulled saltwater taffy, and they all mark off the squares on their kitchen calendars with big red 'Xs,' full of anticipation for red-carpet coronations in the colony. Those worker bees shiver, dance a bit nervously on their legs, grind their mandibles. The anticipation is almost killing them.

Wait.

Just wait.

Be patient now.

Time's up and out she comes, chomping through the wax of her cell roof—shingles torn off—to find her wet wings dry quickly in the new breeze. Antennae twitch, proboscis flickers. She finds the others, pale shadowy queens.

Opens their cells. Kills them, without thought. Instinct is like that, you know.

The old queen leaves a trail of bee blood—this hemolymph—wings torn
like antique wedding veils caught on branches of trees, ribbons of pain,
compound eyes that have dulled themselves in death, sliced open by
the new queen as she clears her way to the throne.

Ascension isn't easy, you know.

Not if you do it right.

iii) Death of the Old Queen

One queen passes the baton to another, tilts her head, shows her daughter
around the hive. Tells her that she can have the decorator re-do the bedroom
in shades of misty violet and smoky grey if that's her dearest longing and wish.

Remember to watch your back, she tells her girl. *You're undoing me,*
as someone else will undo you. You don't believe it now, but it's true.

At that—a sharp inward gasp, then a sigh—a stinger aimed right
at the dorsal heart of the old queen. Fatal strike, daughter kills mother.
Tragic, almost Shakespearean in its essence, all tied up
with a bow after the final, fifth act. Perfect plot graph.

Take a breath, a bathroom break, whatever you need to be okay
with what's just happened here.

It's a lot.

iv) Fancy Funeral, by Royal Decree

Put a fascinator in her hair, instead of a crown. Lay her out on display.

Pass by her funeral bier and toss bits of pansy, lily of the valley, sage,
and red yarrow at her feet. Gather up the snow drops, the squill,
and the clematis flowers. Make of them a bouquet that sings of farewell
and gratitude for services rendered. This colony owes a debt of thanks.

Yes, be sure to put a fascinator in her hair, then, and remind the new queen
to genuflect, to curtsey to her mother's corpse—to note that this is
the very one who gave her life.

The bees will chant, in unison, with flutes and woodwinds
in graceful accompaniment:

The Queen is dead.

Long live the Queen.

(How quickly you've been forgotten …)

v) Courting

Give her four weeks. Then watch:

This new queen goes out to dance at the clubs late on Friday nights. She puts on thigh-high leather boots, paints her face with mascara and lip colour, blushes herself, piles her hair up, and struts her stuff on Elgin Street stages.

She's cool. She's fancy like that.

Truth be told, this new queen is a superstar, a pole dancer, a social media influencer of the highest order. She chameleons herself between inner and outer, between desire and necessity. If you look at her too closely, the glamour will slip, fall to the ground, and she'll fuck you inside out and leave you to die. This queen bee doesn't care if you've got a pet you love, or that your favourite food is pepperoni pizza with mushrooms, pineapple, and anchovies on the side, or that you like winter best. She wants your sperm, so just give it up now. You know you'll love it while it's happening. It's just afterwards that it will hurt.

She'll push you up against the wall of the local bar, in the dark, and then she'll grab you.

You won't be able to let go. You won't want to. That's how it works …

vi) Mating Game

Fancy yourself up then, Queen. Go all stripper tease. Put on the lace
push-up bra, the fuck-me stilettos, the fishnet stockings, those tight
leather shorts. Lean forward, let those drones see what's on offer—buzz,
throb, moan, dance. It's a buffet for the masses and you draw them in,
all magnesium flash, no substance. You're a flash in a pan, a tall flame
that rages, a short life that's all orgasmic at first, but pops and then
sputters out like a candle without oxygen. You're not here for a long time,
just a good time. Your pheromones delude the drones, and maybe even
convince you that life will never end. You're all hairspray and thick makeup
and heels sliding fast and furious on silk sheets at the end of the night.
Gather your sperm while ye may. Assure the continuity of the line.
This is what Darwin wrote about, right? Extinction is a bitch
for some people most of the time.

You gyrate, throb, flash bits and pieces at those drones, fishing
for mates. Take a selfie, now. Don't let a minute go by without
documenting the hunt. After all, the hunt is the thing. Sex them up,
gather that sperm, cast them off to die.

Still, they'll hang around the office door at the end of the day—
those drones—salivating and longing to touch the cool slick of that leather,
that quick whip that you wield dominatrix. You'll drive them to a frenzy
when they can't think except to back you into a corner, hive you up
and down and all around, only to find that you will leave them—
one by one—when the deed is done, endophallus taken in,
broken off, abdomen ripped open.

Death by mating is a graphic film with "White Wedding" playing loudly, over and over in the background.

Cinematic, dramatic, and then—

oh,

so anticlimactic.

vii) Royal Lines

On the first day, she lays so many eggs that she is exhausted by the time
the moon rises above the oak trees, by the time the stars sparkle
in a cobalt blue sky.

Now, here: focus on one simple egg in the centre of a single cell.
She leaves it there. Finds herself dreaming in hexagons,
has nightmares about geometry.

*

On the fourth day, that egg hatches into larva. The workers arrive
and feed it jelly, bolstering its health and helping it to grow.

Be well, little one, they murmur as they spoon the jelly over,
wondering what will come of it.

*

If it has the aspects of a queen, feed it more royal jelly;
if not, just honey and pollen.

Fertilized, it's female—either worker or queen.
Unfertilized, it's male, a drone.

*

Blind larvae squirm, grub around the wax of walls, try to find their sea legs. Can't. Not yet.

Bide your time.

Be patient.

Bide your time.

*

After the sixth day, the workers come, cover the cell with wax.

Seal things up.

Now, in private, the larva hatches.

Now, the bee nurses whisper to themselves, knowing the time has come. You will grow wings, legs, thorax, and abdomen, too.

Now, the magic happens.

Spin yourself around one more time, little bee child. Click your heels together three times and murmur, *There's no place like home. There's no place like home.*

*

On the sixteenth day, she emerges, chewing back that wax,
entering this new world, wondering what comes next. Takes a moment.
Trusts her instincts. Hears Carly Simon singing in the distance,
piped in through loudspeakers at the hive mall.

Now, well, it's all about how nothing stays the same,
and how it's coming around again.

She kills her sisters, then.

'Sororicide' sounds so much nicer than 'murder.'

Ascension isn't easy, you know.

Not if you do it right.

The Pollination Field

The Pollination Field

Plant the seeds. Say their names. Dig into earth.
Your hands and fingers are tools for the future of earth.

Learn of nomenclature, Latin—under fingernails, dirt of earth.
Know origins of seeds. Flora, not fauna. First, this earth.

Second, the fauna—including insects—how they depend on earth.
Plant milkweed, wild bergamot, foxglove beardtongue in earth of field.

Move to verbena, sweet clover, alfalfa, sunflowers. Offer them earth.
Wait for them—with patient faith—to grow, bloom blossom from this earth.

Call pollinators: birds, bats, bees, butterflies, dragonflies, beetles walking earth.
Watch them arrive, on wings and feet, begin the work that springs from earth.

Look at the field, the garden, the foxglove that sways from roots in earth.
Say their names, in English or Latin, in honour of seeds, plants rise from earth.

Apian Architecture

Geometers, these stingless bees
with acid bites, defend a colony
that stretches vertically—
not to be boxed in,
smoked sleepy,
or stunned:

> Nest in hollowed out maples—
> nuzzled in unions where branches
> meet trunks—or else in cracks
> between rocks.

Create honeycombed majesty,
hexagons as holding places—
architectural whimsy spiraling.

> Hives
> grow
> crystalline.
> Worker bees
> follow
> algorithms
> embedded
> deep
> in genes:

this
    waxy
spiral
    reaches
to sky,
    soars
Fibonacci.

These bees as architects
make marks on drafting paper,
quick pencil sketches
before the rising of wings.

Telling the Bees, Cape Sable Island

December 2022

(for Christian Atwood)

Fierce windstorm that lasts the length of three days and nights,
        and news travels fast here.
Lobstering on the Atlantic and pulled over the side
        by an errant wave, nothing kind—

how it rose, crested, pulled him back into itself, vacuum and vortex,
        so he became
more water than fisherman. Boxing Day losses echo up and down
        the shore: cell phones

and socials, big four-wheel drives and quads, people who sit
        with a woman who waits, child
on her knee. Moderate conditions. Four-metre waves.
        Twenty-five-knot winds. Overcast, hungover sea.

Go tell the bees, the ones who hibernate through winter winds,
        avoiding storms and drifting snow. Tell them of the loss—
tragedy, how a young father was swept over,
        sucked in. Lost.

Sleepily, the bees will nudge one another in the hive,
        hum softly through their stupor—recall
bright summer days with seagulls, kids with sand buckets
        and red plastic shovels, sighing.

Somewhere, another lobster boat—chugging towards harbour,
        persistent—brings men back to shore in winter light,
to winding roads, wives and children. Inherited,
        ancient, this life.

Bee Grabbers

Look like a hoverfly, but sting like a bee. *Conopidae.* With your brown wings,
you are chameleon. Come along. Float like a hoverfly, but sting like a bee.
Ambush and then inject your eggs into abdomens of daft bumbles
that suckle flowers mindlessly.

Do you sidle up, sycophantic, to seduce? Do you offer fancy drinks, swizzle
sticks, pink paper parasols for Shirley Temple in a highball glass? No.
You're too blunt for that. You're all *wham, bam, thank you ma'am.*
A zombie apocalypse seems kinder.

Ten to twelve days. Larvae that grow, silent invasive alien, and a bumble
that buries itself—headfirst, head in sand—before it dies. In between,
from start to finish: bee suckles, ignorant of false pregnancy,
internal parasites that mark its end.

Conopidae, you predator. You take what's not yours, plunder, leave
nothing but the hollowed-out bodies of ruined bees, the keen prospects
of lively offspring. Don't look back; your conscience might
catch up to you, turn your ankle. Trip and fall.

Mad Honey

The rhododendrons are wild around the Black Sea, seduce bees
in astronomical configurations, pull them down
to bright blooms—upset orbits & flight patterns.
Imbibe, bees.

Hallucinogenic now, lightheaded, and wondering where the lions go.
Hum along, hedonistic.
Too little, there isn't a buzz. Too much, tip over into something
other than; chase a mirage.

Stagger home with weighted wings, topsy-turvy
and crash mistakenly into colonial hives.
Eager beekeepers build them, nestled in fields of flowers—
know about milk, honey, money.

Mark jars with labels, spidered cursive letters: *deli bal.*
Trade buzzy trips to tourists, priced up.
Whisper quietly. Just a bit. Too much is too much. Mad honey
turns heads, spins pirouette toes.

What draws you in—bee to bloom, mad honey to body
blissed out—can turn you inside out;
floral seduction metamorphosis paints itself in shades
of poison, promises that can't be kept.

Discoscapa apicula

Where do you go to see the ancient bees, the ones
who stung dinosaurs
on Saturday mornings—long before mornings were named
as days of the week?

In museum galleries, well-lit exhibitions of woolly mammoths
and fake savannah
grasslands. The sky is all robin's egg blue, the edges of the wall
an illusion of prehistory.

Myanmar, one hundred million years ago, and a bee
visits a clutch of flowers,
flies haphazardly into clump of tree resin—is ambered for all time.
Beetle larvae on her body.

Fossil bee now, ambered. Beetle larvae are ready to grow,
hatch, pollinate the world
one flower at a time. Prehistoric bees & beetles,
caught in a Polaroid snap.

Google 'fossilized bee' and find New Jersey, Argentina,
and the aforementioned Myanmar. These bees everywhere
before the dinosaurs went away, dragging their DNA
behind them.

Steal it. Un-museum box it. Hang it on a chain—silver grace—
      and then run your finger
down the shape of its curves. Hear it hum, the bee frozen in time,
      longing to fly.

Misery Bay Monarchs

On the edge of Misery Bay, the Manitoulin monarchs soar.
Above my bowed head—broken clouds. They, too, rise to soar.

The radio tells me: all at risk. Reports flock,
monarchs gather at Pelee. Every single one tries to soar.

From here to Mexico, monarchs. For five thousand kilometres.
Who arrives on the Day of the Dead? Souls of lost butterflies soar.

Plant your milkweed quickly now. Don't waste time.
Invasive becomes native. Scientists know fewer monarchs soar.

Plant asters and goldenrod, coneflower and Black-eyed Susans.
Put your hands to the earth, dig deep. Roots can rise to soar.

East Beach, Point Pelee

Walk under Carolinian branches
and the brown ghosts of oak leaves
rustle with the wind, wanting to speak
more loudly. Beyond that, at the place
where more slender trees make an arch
over the trail, the lake a framed photo.

Two red-winged blackbirds call *Marco*
and *Polo* as they sound their way back
to one another. Separated by underbrush,
stray hikers, birdwatchers with binoculars.

On the beach, the skeletons of trees—
sun-bleached whale carcasses—
are made smooth ivory by wind, lake.

Erie is fierce today, waves whipping up on shore,
leaving ice on branches. Down the beach, two geese:
she hangs back, making raspy noises in her throat;
he steps forward into the surf, honking, trying to convince.

Come in!

The water's fine.

The season is about to turn.

Forage

(for Mashkinonje Provincial Park)

Find a marsh, something with a stream running surreptitiously through.
This is the sort of place where you get a soaker if you put your feet in
the wrong spot, where someone will have to offer a hand to help you
cross, where you try to find a rock that rises precarious above
an early spring melt, where you feel the earth softening with
the sensual promise of green. May is advancing. Everything here
is behind in arriving, so go and knock on doors—ask someone
which zone you're in. Look it up online.

In the meantime, find the cattails on your late afternoon walk. Omnipresent,
they rise above low rocks and scrub that hasn't coloured itself in after winter.
In spring, look for tender roots and shoots. Gather, then take them home.

Strip the outside from the inside. Peel layers back to reveal what's at the core:
the hidden story or metaphor that can be boiled, sauteed, fried, or roasted.
Add butter to the pan, a handful of pale white shoots, small ivory bones
swimming in flavour. Salt, pepper, garlic—an open mind.

The stem reveals itself as a cousin to the neighbour's backyard cucumber:
the taste, diluted watercolour after a bout with long Covid; the scent,
the notion of what's been washed away after the snowbanks have gone.

****

Outsides hide insides, so don't tell me
it's easy to decipher what's true,
false, or somewhere in between. Find the plant—
at edge of marsh, hovering mystery.

Falling

(after Mo Hamilton)

Shifts happen slowly, through erosion, over time; the sum of the parts
    is a house sliding
off its foundation—too weak to hold—into a void,
    fast-moving river, or sea.

They will offer you water wings, a flutter board, a pool noodle
    that will never decompose
in a landfill made of waste born of excess. All things will have
    seen better days. Take note.

Built on a concrete base, the feet of the house will age—
    as everything does—sprout corns,
bunions, thickened nails, and joints that shift, too. Strong ankles
    and arches weaken over time.

Concrete wears. No one watches it happen. A corner decays,
    chunks of mortar between red bricks tumble
out when the moon tries on new phases, as calendars turn.
    Put an X there.

Mark the spot of endings and resolutions. And put an X there, too,
    a year or five later,
because erosion is slow. First, bees shiver, the air a frisson
    around wings. Then, a canary falls.

One species goes as another soon takes its place in line.
        They wave goodbye with white
cotton handkerchiefs that were bought in roadside antique shops
        along the eastern shore.

Some things were made to last, sadly: skeleton keys for houses
        full of locks, anchors
and chains for tall ships crossing the Atlantic, greed for land
        that was never ours to misuse.

When the landslide comes, what goes is the worry: a rare bird in Brazil,
        that painted butterfly
from a documentary film, the bee doused in insecticide. The foundation
        is weak. Shore it up.

Milkweed Mourning

(after Sara Angelucci's *Undergrowth*)

Pirouette through wind and rain—ballerina spore—these seeds
        that spin off, ceili bright,
land graceful in tall grasses. Plant themselves
        for next summer's monarchs, bees.

Begin with a solipsistic moth, the one that follows the light
        of the scanner from left to right,
reading lines of energy—flip, flip, flipping towards
        some promised land. Begin there.

Then, conjure the honeybees that travel miles, so certain,
        feed on milkweed in July's heat.
Here first, then off to hive, passing butterflies on wings
        of migration. Which disappears first—

bee, or butterfly? One goes first, without much notice,
        and others follow. Dominoes,
one tumbling into another, nicking edges in quick succession.
        One goes, then another.

Who are you, to stand by silently, without witness? Shame
        is a black velvet dress with broken ribs
ripping through it. Three of Swords: the place where
        the heart used to beat.

Pierced through now—heart—and a voice speaks up to say
          that monarchs, bees, bats,
and beetles tumble through space, shades of their former
          selves before erasure. Smudged.

A Note on the Extinction of Brown Bears in Ireland

The last known brown bear in Ireland lived about 2,500 years ago.
After that, the bears vanished.

When they died, their fur must have curled itself into spirals. It must have
been caught up on the winds coming off the Atlantic. It must have blown
across the Ring of Kerry, down to Beara, and then rolled itself—
dandelion-like—across the sea to the wise steps of the Skelligs.

A scientist marked the bears' paths, places, and migration roads.
They, too, perhaps encountered a famine.

For some bears, deforestation might have meant a journey
to the mountains in search of food and habitation. They may have
danced with faeries or perished in places where the salmon once ran.

Now, in Donegal, there are three brown bears that have travelled far,
from Lithuania. Wildlife sanctuaries and rescue bears behind fences.
Tickets paid and backs of hands stamped.

Extinction happens slowly, maybe while you take a breath
and continue on your way. Before you know it, before you
blink even, you have evolved or become extinct.

Follow the fossils, and you'll find the places where the bears once walked.

Follow the places where their footprints are pressed down
into the earth in ways that mark their passages forever.

The ghosts of the old brown bears weep. They know they cannot return.

Husk

Dead beetle, black husk discarded on lawn—next to dandelion—
conjures ancient Egyptian mummies and mourning dandelions.

You are inherited architecture, insectual and alien at the same time,
torn between dinosaur and postmodern; beside you, a crown of dandelions.

Entomologists turn you over, look under the surface of black armour, wonder
how you survive pandemics, plagues, uncertainty kissed by dandelions.

A child will dress you up, take your empty body, move your limbs as puppeteer,
so you seem alive again, body draped posthumously in a boa of dandelions.

Scientists will undress you afterwards—discard floral tributes, pin you to cork,
place you in a glass box. Museumed, your corpse trails dandelion pollen.

Whale Watching, Vancouver Island
(August 13, 2022)

Near Sooke, rise at dawn and miss sunrise on a grey day.
Sea is silver plated, a tray that presents itself to you—
with handles. What appears is unexpected: fingernail
cuttings, half-moons, a water horse's scalloped tail
swooping up above water line, then down
like a subverted Ferris wheel. You longed for orcas
and now they have arrived, frolicking in surf.

Bears wander between cottages, so you're warned
by staff: mind the paths. Black bear strolled down
to the sea, his huge paws swiping at fallen logs
on the beach, his fur full of twigs and branches.
The man with the bear spray gives it to you—
Just to be safe, you know—then goes on his way.
Stand with your toes in the Strait of Juan de Fuca;
look across to Washington and wonder if orcas
have a nationality, a border to cross, places to be tagged.

Black and white of orca—
dorsal fin, fluke, pectoral flippers—
pinwheels, turning the world upside down.

An Elegy for Australia, Burning

i) K'gari (Fraser Island)

Stand at the edge of the ocean,
under a full moon rising, and then
look up to the Southern Cross, knowing
you'll only see it once in this lifetime.

Stand there, so still, and see a wild dingo
lope furtive along the sand's ragged edge,
its bright eyes reflecting light as it spots you—
dashes into undergrowth, where it's most safe.

Lightning strike in November, and that spark catches,
ruins the wildest parts of paradise—so that some dingoes
disappear, vanish into greenery that burns too bright
to speak of survival. So many calendar days, up in flames.

ii) New South Wales

An ecologist says eight thousand koalas have died,
trapped high in the eucalyptus branches—
the leaves so flammable, filled with oil—
and those trees have gone up like bright fountains,
fierce fireworks, so out of control.

The kangaroos rush ahead of the flames,
try to outrun the impossible. Days later—
after the firestorm has passed—they are found,
charred statues of bodies caught up in wire fences,
echoes of a shadowed nightmare, coloured in inferno.

iii) Hollowed-out things

Here are the online photos of hollowed-out things:
a woman clinging to her man, arms wrapped tightly
around his torso, a silent sob so frozen, captured on film;
orphaned koalas, fur burned from the skin around their eyes,
gaze vacant and frightened, sheltered in a laundromat;
someone kneeling, against a blood-red sky,
weeping for the loss of her husband and son;
tourists stranded on a beach, trapped by highest flames,
waiting for rescue from a ship that sails ocean waves.

A heart—your own broken heart—such a hollowed-out thing.

iv) Condolences

And we will sit, in our quiet January places,
with winter snowbanks & eavestrough icicles,
and wonder what we should do:
shake our heads, confounded, shocked by the stories;
say 'horrible, horrible' and then make a pot of tea;
send notes via email to friends in New South Wales,
asking if they're well, and hoping to hear they are;
scan social media feeds, donating to save koalas,
knowing—all the while—that this is only the beginning.

v) Out of control

You are 'out of control,' a fire that spreads on one
or more fronts, an uncontained perimeter, a prayer
that someone speaks quietly in the middle of the night.

You are place names on a map in a country I once visited,
home to hills and fields filled with wallabies and kangaroos
that jumped next to the path where I walked, peering curiously
at me and keeping their distance in pre-dawn light.

You are 'out of control,' and my stomach turns at the thought,
of how the planet warms because of us, and how we turn away,
shuffle our feet, think our own burning times will not arrive.

Slag Dump

Something to set your watch by, the way they poured the slag out
over the ridge, and how the house sat on the edge of the hill—
named Wembley Drive—and how you would turn off the lights
in the kitchen so we three or four kids could kneel on the metal top
of the table and widen our eyes to take in the scene. Better than
fireworks, the slag's glow. The sky lit up as if a giant were using
orange crayons to scrawl a line above the horizon.

What was it? Leftovers, you told us, chuckling. Pieces of ore,
melting together, poured like lava down that hill. Later,
friends would have slag as driveway, pay for bits of black rock
to surface the roughest of gravel, stop the dust from rising
without warning when you backed up the car.

In winter, the slag would melt the snow, leave a trail—
first red and orange, then black and cooled, as if it had never
even snowed. In daylight, there wasn't a glow. In daylight,
there was scorched earth, and a smokestack that belched out
detritus, raining acid on cars, metal stair railings, concrete steps.
My toqued head.

Telling the Bees

Queen Anne's Lace
(after Andrea Kowch)

They have mistaken her hair for a hive,
these bees that hover, buzz in her ears.
She holds wild carrot—the plate from which they dine;
solitary queen, her floral tribute a hive.
Look away. She is mistress of all she surveys.
Bees will arrive, planes to an airfield as they land.
They have forgotten what wildness is. Their hive
is a chimera, hair transformed, buzzing between ears.

Gathering the Clay

Three thousand years ago, you put your hands down deep into thick Nile mud,
let your fingers scoop it up, closing your eyes as you touched
essence of earth, the place of beginnings. From your cradle to coffin,
you gathered clay for honeybee hives, food for the king's tomb—
the pyramid still hovering geometric above that far horizon.

Honey for a boy king, face masked with gold and indigo.
Left as gift for the world to come. Millennia later, some man dressed
in khaki opened a door, brushed dust from his hands, found the jar.
Archaeologists huddled, opened the lid, dipped their fingers.

Ancient honey still sweet, they marvelled
how you went down to the river, dug your hands down deep
into the muck of clay. How you gathered dung, straw, and mud
to fashion tubes for bees that would soon die, but leave
behind the honey for the king's crossing.

Attic Colony

Fierce gusts of rain—slanting diagonal,
against gravity's pull—pelt a Pennsylvania house
battered by wind. Hard blown enough that a hand
placed on the rattle of a front-hall doorknob
would feel a rush of weather yank vampirical,
trying to get in without invitation.

Upstairs, the secret colony tucked up under the shingles
floods, water and honey mixing up a fancy potion—
mead spilling out over edges of comb.
Drunken bees swim over wax, honey, bodies,
following path of least resistance. Nowhere
to dry their wings, sodden with loss.

The attic is a throbbing migraine.
The dog in the downstairs front hall goes mad—
pacing out relentless, patterned circles—
stopping only to lick sweet rivers running down walls
and baseboards. Drags his massive paws
through pools of honey on hardwood.

Queen Bee in a Tiny Yellow Box

In London, a man carries a queen bee in a tiny yellow box. He holds her close, carefully, his palms curled around that box as if she is the last queen bee left alive on the planet. She may be, for all he knows. He holds her close, carefully, lifting that tiny yellow box high above his head, his arms extended as if in a modern dance move—arched, curving, buttressed, graceful.

The previous queen has abdicated—
    without warning—
        leaving her colony in tatters.

One day, the others wake up, sense her absence as newly announced presence; stir and swirl. At first, they continue to dance ordered pavanes—pretending that she hasn't gone. Their quasi-Elizabethan dance is full of sharp and courteous bows from the waist, and then a frenzy of fast wings that beat out a rhythm only they can hear.

Her scent gone, they spiral into buzzing dissension, bumping into one another around corners of the hive, trying to find the clearly illuminated exit sign. Confused, stymied, or just longing to mate—the drones don't know what to make of her departure. They bump up against each other, longing and not finding what they search for. Desperation in the longing that leads to a sharp-edged and serrated emptiness. Longing without satisfaction: the definition of futility.

They swarm, the colony, around a bicycle stand in Hackney—covering the seat of the locked bike, lining the spokes of its back wheel. Two wheels and how many bees, exactly? Two wheels going nowhere and how many bees buzzing, now? Two wheels that are immobilized, but still writhing with movement of wings and antennae. Ready to race off at a moment's notice, this bike that is covered in insects.

Two wheels. And … how many bees … exactly?

This new queen, so solitary, and yet bejeweled, restless in her desire for a mate or two. Or more. Polyamorous. She nestles, in that tiny yellow box, held up—reverent and divine—high, high above the man's head, rustles her wings, admiring her body as she looks back towards thorax and abdomen. Surely, she thinks, they will desire her. Surely, they will court her. Surely, she will lay the eggs that will win accolades for generations to come. And then, then, they will drape bright garlands of paper and wax-woven bunting around her, so that she is up high—on a pedestal—as a true, queenly bee ought to be. She will become a lighthouse for the lost colony, calling home the workers and the drones, and longing for satisfaction that might never be found.

Swarm

When she was small (the very smallest of the small) she remembered
seeing a nest of wasps perched high, high up under the eaves.
Her grandfather had poked at it with a broomstick—thinking of Germany,
patriarchy, and other unspoken sharp things—and she had pulled back
and in, made herself smaller than small could ever
be outside her own imagination.

He had poked, poked, poked at that papery grey nest. From high up,
from beyond six feet tall, he raised his arms long and lanky,
far far far up above, grunting and cursing under his breath.

She had pulled back and in. She had made herself small,
smaller than small could be.

*

A whimper, deep inside her chest. A whine. A worry.
The swarming. The screaming.

His voice, booming, *Don't move. Don't run.*
Don't scream. STAND STILL.

But she, smallest of the small girls, ran. Ran hard, ran fast, ran far—
her legs spinning like windmills in that book about tulips and windmills
in Holland. Or like the shiny little pinwheels that you could hold up
high high high above your head in brisk wind. They would flash
sparkles in front of your eyes, they would, until you wanted
to spin dizzy around and around and then collapse on the grass
laughing—with dandelions or rough daisies woven into your hair.

She ran. All the way home.
They followed her.

*

He poked the nest of wasps, stubborn man that he was. Got stung
over and over again. Served him well. Couldn't tell the difference
between wasps and bees, someone said later, shaking their head.
Didn't know that wasps survived after stinging, but bees didn't.
Maybe should've picked on the bees after all …

*

For years afterwards, she ran from wasps, danced minuets of avoidance
with bees, remembering the stings and the buzzing. Then, one day,
when she was bigger, a grown up, she watched a bee bumbling
in a poppy, hovering and buzzing with baritone beauty. Not so scary,
she told her littler self; not so scary after all.

Telling the Bees

(after the Irish tradition of telling the bees of a death in the family)

The morning his wife lost their littlest one,
not even born yet, the beekeeper went
out into the long back field with
a slim black ribbon.

Just the size of a minute,
that tiny one passed out of
her worn womb like a
half-formed semi-colon—
a pause taken between breaths
without thinking.

And so, he went out into that back field,
with the curl of dark silk clutched
tightly in his closed hand: an offering.

He went out, then, into that long green field,
past the still-sleeping cows that must
mostly dream of the moon. Only the
curlews, circling high up in the sky,
watched him go beyond the gate.

He walked, one foot in front of the other,
sucking in air like a bellows
before it smokes a hive.

When he reached the hive at dawn,
the sun rising over the hills behind him,
he told the bees with tears in his eyes,
wrapped the colony with the ribbon.

They listened, flew up to dry his tears,
offered him a chanted dirge in return.

Sainted

(for Gobnait)

You came from Clare,
but the sixth-century clerics
didn't record your work.
Men erased you before you could
even find a spare pen,
write things down.

Instead, they tried to pretend you didn't live at all,
a woman as patron saint of bees and beekeepers.

They said that you did not build a church
on the rocky shore of Inisheer. An angel
never told you to go inland, find a spot
for your own resurrection. And those fine white deer
at Ballyvourney were only ever about
a witchy spell in Munster—not a place to build
and lead women mystics in a land ruled by
such bent and pickled men.

*

Thieves ransacked your monastery,
and you sent them the gift of a charm:
a swarm of hot bees readied, fierce.

Gobnait, the ruins of your church
still stand on Inisheer—
ancient rocks and stones—
wild weather and ocean worn.
In Cork, a stained-glass likeness
colours you tall and proud, dressed in blue,
a pale hand extended in reckoning.

Flick of your finger.
                Flutter of bees' wings.

        Your stings all stung—
                in good conscience.

        Your soul, a bee rising,
                resurrected.

Skellig Michael

"The bee is more honoured than other animals, not because it labours, but because it labours for others."
~Saint John Chrysostom

These monks, like honeybees—
industrious, steadfast, and keen—
genuflecting to ocean and sky,
carrying stones up high stairs
to build their hived huts—
hoping to find heaven
in honeyed prayer.

*

In high places, it is easier to
stretch your arm—far, far, far up—
let your fingertips touch cumulus clouds
and caress the face of what's unseen,
gather it to you as you would a lover.
Try to map its weather clearly on the
curved back wall of your skull,
in blue ink or pencil, to be returned to
later, in memory, when the inside of that
ivory wall is worn by time, weather, loss.

Knocks on the Beehive

When he goes, the man who cared for you
for so many years, his son—likely not his daughter—
will walk up through the long fields and stop at your hive,
knock quietly to let you know that your keeper has gone on.

You will stop, certainly, and still your wings,
wait for trace or drop of dew on hexagonal wax of hive door,
and thrum your thorax in grief, waggle this way and that
to show that he is wished well on his journey.

A few knocks, then, and the keeper passes from father to son,
from this one to that, from generation to generation,
so that colonies continue even while keepers disappear.
Bees carry on beyond the humans—paint the world in pollen, not pain.

Dundurn Beetles

Gave up their bodies, crushed and powdered,
        to blooms of colour: carmine—
for robes of kings, double-backed red chesterfields,
        colour of curtains.

That chesterfield, centre of the crimson-tufted
        drawing room, colour of blood.
Back to back: one looks out to lawn, the other
        to hearth's coloured fire.

The laird's domain, red the mark of aristocracy;
        the colour of colonials who dig down
into Burlington Heights, build up, disturb lands—
        colour of blood.

Beetles gave up their lives for Dundurn's red front room,
        blooms of colour where they once
roamed free. Sacrificial décor, carapaces crushed
        to red velvet.

Shut the heavy wooden door, quietly. Ghosts of beetles
        dance, crimson, and family shades pace
the carpet, not knowing which century
        is coloured *now*.

Teir Bheach

"Ask the wild bee for what the druid knew."
~a phrase from ancient Scottish lore

To sleep in the back garden,
one arm across your own breasts,
the other out from your side, drifting
like a curved bow or sculpted line of waist.

From above, from the sky,
you will look—perhaps to a high crow—
like an ivory crescent moon, your pale skin
blushed by late morning sun.

To close your eyes and rest,
in rough and imperfect summer grasses;
to hear the hum of a bee's wings
fluttering at your ear.

One hand across your chest,
another with fingers that point
loosely to your feet—
open to elements and possibility:

your heart and feet
will guide you.

Your Soul Is a Bee

Some night, lay yourself down in that field,
as if giving yourself to a lover—opened, free.

Let your fingers dig deep down into the turf, so peat
gets under your nails—composts you before you know it.

Sleep soundly, now. The earth will embrace you whole,
the wind will cross you in wet-dazzle from the sea—holy.

That old woman passing on the road sees you there,
just before dawn. Watches a tiny bee exit your mouth.

She remembers, if you ask her, how the soul is a bee that
rises from the body—how it leaves one home for another.

Cortege

Once

(after Vijay Seshadri)

The real story of my life is the story of its bereavement.
If I wrote that story now, it would be full of soul,
how mine forgot its body and wanted to escape. About how it watched
people go—leave—one after the other, like a row of pinned socks on
a clothesline caught up in a windstorm, disappearing into gusty ether.
Once I was unruly, just a mind like a wild pencil scribble that went beyond
its parameters, until it found a medication to save it. No clear margins.
Once I was a blessing, and then I was a curse, and then I tore open skin
to become wound, and the wound healed. A blessing,
            a survival story that kept on keeping on.
And one late January afternoon, before St. Brigid's Day arrived on the back
of a coal-black crow with a ragged wing, I spoke in curses rather than in
italicized litanies, and I spoke in ancient witch's spells rather than in rosaries,
            and I spoke in agony rather than in sacramental holies.
The real story is about bereavement and how nothing gold can ever stay
(because Frost was right) and how sometimes the crack *is* how the light
gets in (because Cohen was also right) and how the two might somehow
marry one another when we turn our heads and look the other way—
            a climax that gives birth to something other than bereavement.
Once I stood under a pine tree at Recollet Falls, looked up into a blue-grey
sky, blinked three times, hid the blur of loss, the tenderness of this fierce
weather, fierce heart. The Canadian Shield, one solitary crow, the French River.

In the Bag I Brought Home from Palliative Care on the Night My Mother Died

The memory of her voice when she was well, singsong
and Ottawa Valley descended; her laugh, pealing

like a bell, joyful, at noon on a Thursday, counting out twelve,
even though she died in the evening;

a blue-lined recipe card with a note about chicken and dumplings—
don't measure, just use your hand, fingers, a pinch and not a teaspoon;

her brown eyes; long, graceful fingers on hands that played
songs from *West Side Story*;

her stories, remembered, and that I should have written down
on paper, where they could be kept, safe;

lilacs, peonies, California poppies, and peppermint—for smelling,
or putting in iced tea on hot July days;

a paperback mystery, the page corner bent big, her bookmark
left behind—never used.

The Sadness is on Me

The fossilized cloves that nail themselves
into the thick peel of my mother's orange pomander
mummify any suggestion of decay or loss.

Starred constellations imprint themselves
into flesh of thumb, pad of index finger,
rind of citrus. Blend of sweet tang
and pungent spice wafts through
the long bedroom closet that housed
weathered cotton and inherited wool.

Still, after she died, tiny wings fluttered down
from her favourite sweater—dried hydrangea petals,
notes sent from some far-off place as we packed up her clothes
into tattered cardboard boxes and spare plastic grocery bags.

Memory Box

Death is an impossible meadow and the memory
of your voice has slipped away through its long grasses,
hidden rabbit holes—places where spiders and ants
mourn the bodies of dead bees.

In this ancient prayer book, you pressed spring violets
and pansies to dry for later. You forgot the petals, flattened
between two holy cards: one of a handsome Jesus, the other
of Mary—hovering turquoise above the world.

A green Irish Connemara marble worry stone, place worn out
for my thumb to find a home, something that fits in the palm of
my hand on a rainy day, making me long for some past life on
the banks of the Shannon, near sheep and sound of water rushing.

A pebble from the shore of Vancouver Island, not stolen, but borrowed,
and how I wonder how old it is—before Christ or after? If I touch
my tongue to it, would I taste the Pacific's tears? (But salt
is without taste in a pandemic year with long Covid.)

Slim stick of selenite, milky white. Hold it up to the light and imagine
angels sliding down the banister of its geological grain, falling with
a thump into a pile of spare feathers. Temperance, upended,
pouring Earl Grey from one cup into another.

An engagement photo of my maternal grandmother. She looks like
the young Queen—beautiful!—all pearls, tailored twinset, and a far-off
look in her eyes. My grandmother was married in the coronation year,
but she never made it onto a coffee mug. May 1937.

One of my mother's wild hippie rings—amber and silver—
the one I can't bear to put on my finger. If I look down too quickly,
without thinking, I see her hands and not mine.
Her fingers, not mine.

Replacement

Your father's metal knees, upended from
thick plastic bags—dust of cremains on rug—
and you held them up, titanium spheres
cradled in the open palms of your hands,
a man with the face of a boy, hidden.
I'm holding my father's knees, you said,
lifting them up high, as if crystal balls
rather than replacements for worn-down joints.
Your eyes, Atlantic, fill with sudden tears,
threatening to fall. Close up now, pull in,
your heart too open, lotus blooming from muck;
gather up the wet towels from tub, shake out
the kitchen mat and hang as offering
to back porch gods. You hope to forget grief.

Moonlight over Lawrencetown, Summer 1998

Just twenty-seven: pretty, but she didn't think so, bogged down
by problems with skin that freckled and pimpled without warning;
curious, but terrified, driving cross-country with a boy she fancied—
physicist and star gazer; wondering where she'd end up by thirty, forty-five,
fifty-two, spinning a fortune teller's glass ball in the palms of her hand, magic.

Scent of salt water, brine, and seaweed steeped, and socks
shedding grains of sand in the car, and everything lit up ivory.
Even the ocean knew it had a story on its hands, watching
the two of them on the beach—bums on sand,
knees side by side, like kids out after curfew.

A penny for your thoughts—a copper cent
with a queen's head on one side, maple leaf
on the other; seaside colony, this province,
all tartan and bagpipes, youth and love lost.

Give her a cent to spend,
if you ever thought she was precious,
worth more than a penny cast
out of copper—an opened oyster shell.

Vintage Wedding Gown

(after Galway Kinnell)

Here my mother's wedding gown, hanging in yellowed plastic
        in the front closet.
Here I touch crisp plastic cover and think *This is not for me ...*
        Text my sister a simple note: *This, this is yours.*
Here from between forgotten winter coats, hold it up
        to the light and imagine what she must have looked like,
        in November 1968: snow on the ground, bridesmaids with beehives,
        and white bouquets with yellow ribbons that sang against the navy
        of her best church coat.
Here I finger the pearl buttons—tiny, half-globes of ivory—
        wonder if she'd kept it for one of us, or both.
Here I see that she was much tinier, didn't have the sculpted
        slopes of my hips, the hills and valleys of my breasts.
Here I wonder if marriage had suited her, beyond the day she wore
        the pretty dress. All yellowed silk. We sold our family house
        and took apart the leftover memories of our parents' lives—
        bundled everything into Rubbermaid bins that would live
        in the basement, unopened for years. Wounds, trauma, love.
Here I fold it gently, fingers stroking the place where her shoulders once
        filled fabric, before I even knew her. Before I was born.
Here I recall Jackie Kennedy, the dress she wore like this one, with a matching
        pillbox hat and tall, silk-covered pumps. My mother was a mirror,
        dressed up for a wedding, longing for love. Later, the dress became
        a footnote, a marker in a life that was once hopeful, then not.

Here I find that weddings don't matter, but dresses do—green velvet
or vintage empire waists, fit and flare. Wonder more about whether
they have pockets than if some imaginary daughter will inherit them
after I die. I imagine daughters in other dimensions, ghosts from
my own body's better days.

Sea Road Visitation
(August 13, 2022)

The ocean, calm pewter,
and the orcas come in
to feed, fins up—cartwheels—
my eyes, soft, searching.

A country away—
months, too—
and the calendar marks
the day with certainty.

I'll send you the essence
of an orange dahlia in
a clear glass vase, the peace
of orcas turning the sea over
and over, looking for fish,
searching.

Cairdeas

(for Laura-Leigh)

Just before dawn, the orcas arrive,
turn themselves upside down in soft rain,
half circles of shadow against silver
in Pacific's mirror—a Juan de Fuca flash.
Your two birds, on canvas, are still,
caught in brush stroke, branches of berried tree.
Kindreds sit next to one another, brush away
tears, eyes magpie bright, feathers ready to fly.

I look out the wide ferry window,
sailing over the Salish Sea—
full of painted sailboats, gulls, and seals—
write broken sonnets about the ocean, mountains,
wonder if leaving Departure Bay means
choosing not to arrive anywhere else.

Cortege

Rose petals, fallen, pieces of torn confetti, carried
offerings on backs of ants, left around bee's spent body.

Spent bee body, and petals carried as offering
but the carcass blocks the entry to ant nest.

Blocks entry to nest—this carcass—so the ants rally,
carry more fragments, hope to store food for winter.

Storing food for winter, fragments of flowers carried,
but the corpse prevents migration, transportation.

The corpse prevents migration, stops up the tunnel; no transport
is possible. And winter hovers, waiting, as leaves turn shades.

Leaves turn, shades of themselves, waiting as winter hovers.
Perfume rises as the petals fall, fragrance in a sealed envelope.

This fragrance in a manila envelope—sealed, but not sent.
Perfume rises, rose petals fall, flutter. Torn confetti.

Windsor Bats

(for Jane and David)

You take me to see Windsor bats at dusk—
when they dip under Willistead trees,
relying on chirps, songs, and screeches to speak
to one another beneath the trees.

I stand, silent, arms at my side—palms open—
head tilted and looking up into trees,
and you two crane necks, adjust gazes, raise fingers
to point at dark of tree branches.

Paired, birds who only move together, you shift into
and out of tree trunk auras.
Coupled, two magpies that never part, your union
is anchored in joining of limbs to tree.

You smile, see me scrunch up, knowing bats soar high
above in Carolinian trees, not bothering
with poets walking behind friends who are lovers paired—
two birds in a tree.

Windsor bats, pollinators on parade, swoop through dusk
to eat mosquitoes hiding in trees.
Crouch down! In nightdark, bats weave ribbons in sky,
chirp path to limbs of tree: there, now.

Third Tale:
Coda—A Bee Reflection

i) Afterbirth

Go to the ocean, first to the west and then to the east. Bookend the passage with solace of sea, whales and shipwrecks, selkies and their cousin mermaids, seaweed and lobster fishermen. To the west, Vancouver Island and Shawnigan Lake dawn swims. To the east, feeding a wood fire stove that fuels a Sambro house perched on the edge of the Atlantic, so that the Irish wolfhound stays warm on Boxing Day. Hold on tight so the wind doesn't pick you up and fling you out towards the Grand Banks.

The beekeeper was untrue, all smoke and mirrors. It comes—to all good women tricked by too-handsome-men—the very notion that they were used solely for comfort, solace, safe harbour. Shake your heads, now. Sure, they're all fancy talkers, quick to arrive and then quicker out the front door.

Out there, way past the Sambro lighthouse, so many fishermen lost,
some as young as the peach fuzz that sprouted on their chins,
above their lips. The depth of loss is greater than the depth
of the sea, no matter where you measure from.

Don't go out to the sea, boys. Raise bees instead.

I wished they'd just gone trouting instead, stayed on a lake
rather than go out to sea. The lobsters won't remember them,
but the people will.

ii) You Will Get Stung

Try as you might, you will get stung. Pretend not to care.
    Pretend that it is only a flesh wound.
One sting won't hurt, mind. A hundred would be lightning striking
    all at once, your body on fire.

Stinging is a last resort, a defence against invasion or upset.
    A sting means a drone's death. Mating, too.
So many suicidal tendencies, programmed
    to work, dance, buzz, mate.

Trying to avoid being stung is pointless. Would you walk in fear,
    or in love? Instead, lean in close, smell lemongrass
on the queen's wings, suss out her centre—
    pulse points for continuing.

iii) Smoke and Mirrors

Good beekeepers manage bees, even knowing that
the notion of control is an illusion.

So much illusion, Beekeeper:
you were an actor bound for London stages—
with excellent lighting and your own artistic director—
but sidestepped to the northeast, ruining people as you came,
leaving spent bodies in your wake. Lies of omission are lies
just the same, but you smoke the bees into submission,
seducing them with blue eyes and a low, measured voice.

What happens when the smoker dies? What then?

iv) There Comes a Time

When the woman walks down from the glade, the wax torn away
from her eyes—so that she can see clearly, not be deceived. Thought maybe
she needed the beekeeper, to free her, to help her move. But beekeepers know
how to use smoke, to billow it out, blinding once-wise witches so that they can
no longer see. Take away sight, what's left? Second sight. Take away
the glade, what's left now? Travel. Go beyond the bend in the road.

Here's what she couldn't see, but now does:

Look for the pods of orcas in the Salish Sea. Don't find them. Zodiac hunters,
cameras ready, scanning surface as if it's canvas—ready to be painted acrylic.
As if it's sky instead of salt water. Remember the story of the woman who
went swimming, saw bubbles rising from underneath. Her face became
a question mark, until the humpback rose, ruining her breaststroke.
She swam away, frightened by the shock, never returned to the sea to swim.

Once burned, twice shy.

v) But Follow Your Heart

To where the music is floating up above the meadow, the yard, the little patch of grass—a ribbon of sound that has led you to the hive.

There, you see, the forager bees dream of their youth, think of band stands, Count Basie, Ella Fitzgerald, and sparklers on the Fourth of July, and how Sadie Hawkins dances were nightmares for wallflowers, but good
for bees ... if wallflowers were willing.

And the bees murmur,

mumble,

even bumble,

wonder if the dance floor will still be there

in the morning

or if

it will have disappeared with the

rising of the sun

over that field that stretches out

beyond

beyond

beyond

Notes

The title of the first section, "First Tale: The Queen in the Bee-Loud Glade," alludes to the "bee-loud glade" in William Butler Yeats's poem, "The Lake Isle of Innisfree." My undergraduate thesis project was centred on Yeats's poetry, so I have loved and admired him and his work for decades. Thanks to my great-aunts, Norah and Maureen Kelly, for introducing me to this poem, but also to Laurence Steven, for his third-year Modern Poetry course at Laurentian University back in the early 1990s, where I became transfixed with the notion of reading all of Yeats's work. (It took longer than just one year, but I got there!)

Three poems, "Winter at Peggy's Cove, Nova Scotia," "Stings," and "Cortege," are all inspired by Jericho Brown's duplex form. I learned this form from Yvonne Blomer in her class on poetic line and form at the Metchosin International Summer School of the Arts (MISSA) on Vancouver Island in Summer 2022. The Poetry Foundation defines Brown's duplex form as "a poetic form … that subverts or is a 'mash up' of older poetic forms, such as the pantoum, the sonnet, and the ghazal." He first used it in his third collection, *The Tradition* (Copper Canyon Press, 2019), which won the Pulitzer Prize for Poetry in 2020.

The poem "Code" includes an italicized line of marine signals. The order in which they appear on that initial line corresponds to the order of the messaging lines as they descend the page under that first line. The International Code of Signals is a system of internationally recognized maritime signal flags that are linked to specific letters and messages. Marine vessels can use these signals to communicate.

"Swim at Own Risk" (after Carolyn Forché) is inspired by Forché's poem "Toward the End."

The poem "Itinerary" (after Roo Borson) is inspired by Borson's poem "Solstice" which she begins writing with the address, "As for you, world—". I have echoed that with "As for you, Dragonfly …" at the start of my poem. The first line also includes my phrase "you leave the island in the middle of the night," which is a reference to the content of another Borson poem, "Leaving the Island."

The poem "Mad Honey" was inspired by three essays that I read online. The first, "The Strange History of 'Mad Honey,'" was written by Emma Bryce and published in *Modern Farmer* on September 4, 2014. The second, titled "Mad honey," was written by David J. Evans and published in *The Apiarist* on September 28, 2018. The third, titled "What it's like tripping on mad honey, the hallucinogen that (maybe) is an aphrodisiac," was written by Niko Vorobyov, and published in the April 10, 2022 issue of *Salon*. Mad honey is found in Turkey and is referred to as *deli bal*. According to Bryce's essay, the reddish honey "contains an ingredient from rhododendron nectar called grayanotoxin—a natural neurotoxin that, even in small quantities, brings on light-headedness and sometimes, hallucinations."

"Apian Architecture" is a poem that was inspired by my research around the Australian stingless bee that is known as *Tetragonula carbonaria*. Two articles that I found helpful in my research were Brandon Specktor's "Nobody Knows Why These Bees Built a Spiral Nest," published in *Live Science* on January 22, 2018, and Elaina Zachos's piece "Why These Stingless Bees Build Spiral Hives," published on the National Geographic website on February 2, 2018. These bees are referred to colloquially as "sugarbag bees." Specktor says that "out of about 20,000 known bee species around the world, *T. carbonaria* is one of only 500 without stingers."

"Bee Grabbers" is a poem about conopids (from the family *Conopidae*) or thick-headed flies. These flies are black and yellow in colour and are parasitoids. As Athayde Tonhasca says on her blog on Scottish pollinators, in an article titled "Thick-headed undertakers" dated May 20, 2021, many conopids are wasps and flies. They are referred to as "bee grabbers" because they latch onto a host (in this case a bumblebee) and lay their eggs into the body of the host. The host (in this case, the bee) continues to live until the conopid's larvae hatch. At that point, the larvae destroy the host.

"Falling" (after Mo Hamilton) is an ekphrastic piece based on artist Mo Hamilton's exhibit of linocut prints titled the *100 Houses Project*. The poem is inspired by the image presented in a print of the same name. In Hamilton's "Falling," there is the image of a linocut house sliding from the land and into water. The notion of erosion, and of how humans often damage the natural environment without thought, is central to the poem as a warning for us to be guardians of the environment—and of the health of all its creatures, plants, land, and water.

"Milkweed Mourning" (after Sara Angelucci's *Undergrowth*) is an ekphrastic piece that takes its inspiration from one of Angelucci's images. A tiny moth is caught moving through the image, so here is a reference to a pollinator, but also to the role of milkweed as a plant that helps pollinators to flourish in a world where so many bee species are at risk of extinction.

The poem "Queen Anne's Lace" (after Andrea Kowch) is an ekphrastic piece that is inspired by Michigan artist Andrea Kowch's painting of the same name. In Kowch's painting, the bees hover above the blooms, again referencing the links to the various plants and flowers that pollinators depend upon.

The poem "Gathering the Clay" was inspired by my readings around the role of bees in ancient Egypt, and particularly of the story about how a jar of honey was found when archaeologists opened King Tutankhamun's tomb in 1922. For the ancient Egyptians, honeybees had a spiritual and religious significance, moving between worlds. The bee hieroglyph became the symbol for Lower Egypt. The beekeepers of the time kept bees in tubes of clay and mud taken from the Nile. These tubes were often stacked in pyramid formations put on rafts and moved from place to place along the river to ensure pollination of different types of flowers throughout various seasons. The Planet Bee Foundation website was helpful to my research about ancient Egyptian bees and beekeepers, as well as the article, "How People Practiced Beekeeping in Ancient Egypt," which can be found on the Live Beekeeping website.

The notion of "Telling the Bees" is one that finds its origin in ancient Celtic and European traditions. In Ireland, the Brehon laws began to be codified between 438-441 AD, and the Bee Judgements (*Bechbretha*) were part of those laws. Bees were so important in ancient Ireland that they were considered a part of the family. If someone died, one of the remaining family members needed to go out to the hive and tell the bees. This practice is also referred to in another poem, "Knocks on the Beehive." In Celtic mythology, the presence of a bee near a body soon after a person's physical death symbolized the soul leaving the body. This is reflected in my poem "Your Soul Is a Bee." Interestingly, another Irish story has the appearance of any tiny, white moth or butterfly as a visitation by someone you've loved and who has died and gone on to the spirit world.

"Sainted" (for Gobnait) is a poem for St. Gobnait, the patron saint of bees and beekeepers. February 11 is her feast day. Her shrine is at Ballyvourney, County Cork, Ireland. I was inspired by Gobnait's story, by the beautiful stained-glass window in the Honan Chapel, University College Cork, made by Harry Clarke (1889-1931), and by her life. Gobnait was a sixth- or seventh-century abbess and healer, someone who helped to heal others. Many speculate that she used honey as a healing salve. She moved from Clare to Inisheer, where she established a church, and then kept on to Ballyvourney, where she established an abbey. She was also said to have sent her bees out to defend Ballyvourney against English invaders at one point, and this endeared her to the Irish.

"Skellig Michael" is a poem that speaks to the old Irish monastery off the west coast of Ireland. Dating back to the sixth or seventh century AD, Skellig Michael is known for its harsh landscape and climb to the top, but also for the beehive-shaped huts that the ancient monks built. These huts protected the monks from the elements, certainly, but they also echoed the structures that beekeepers would have used in Ireland at that time. Bees, in both pagan and Christian Ireland, were revered for being symbols of wisdom, perhaps because they seemed to live meditative and ordered lives within their hives, and because they moved as winged messengers (like birds, or other insects with wings) between land and sky—between body and spirit. I read Philip Kosloski's blog post "Why did the monks on Skellig Michael make huts shaped like bee hives?" and Emma Donoghue's brilliant novel, *Haven,* to get a sense of this liminal place.

"Dundurn Beetles" is a poem that specifically references Hamilton's Dundurn Castle (1835) and captures a visit I had there with a friend in October 2022. Throughout the guided tour, I wondered why the history of the house didn't also reference the Indigenous peoples who lived there prior to the house's construction. Dundurn Castle is the house that Sir Allan Napier MacNab built for himself. He was a railway magnate, lawyer, and also served as Premier of the United Canadas (1854–1856). The drawing room is awash in the colour red, so I began to research how cochineal beetles were often harvested to provide colour for carmine, the deep red fabric so often used by upper-class British settlers at that time. This is the same colour that is used to make ceremonial robes for the British aristocracy.

"Ceir Bheach," in Irish and Scottish Gaelic, translates to "beeswax" in English.

The poem "The Sadness is on Me" is the English translation of the Irish Gaelic phrase, *tá brón orm*. Pádraig Ó Tuama, the noted Irish poet and theologian, suggests that the Irish phrase means that we do not become emotions, but that they pass over (or are just visiting) us for brief periods of time. We are not defined solely by passionate emotions; they pass just as weather might travel across a stormy sky.

"Once" (after Vijay Seshadri) was inspired by Seshadri's poem "Memoir." In that poem, Seshadri starts his second sentence with "The real story of a life," and repeats the word "Once" a couple of times in the poem. My first line begins "The real story of my life" and I use the repetition of the word "Once" more than a few times in my poem.

"Vintage Wedding Gown" is inspired by Galway Kinnell's poem, "The Road Between Here and There."

"Cairdeas" is an ekphrastic poem that I wrote for my friend Laura-Leigh Gillard. It's written in the form of a broken sonnet. The word cairdeas is an Irish and Scottish Gaelic word that means friendship. The poem is based on a painting that Laura created for me as a gift. It features two magpies sitting on a branch together. Magpies are one of my favourite birds, and her painting is an allusion to the magpies that make an appearance in my earlier poetry collection, *These Wings.* Laura sat with me for several days in the early part of 2022, offering her steadfast friendship during what was one of my more difficult times in life. I wrote "Cairdeas" as a birthday gift for her later that same year, to thank her for being there for me.

"Cortege" is a poem that was inspired by some research I did around ants and how they dispose of their dead. In this case, there was a video online, posted by Managing Editor of *IFL Science*, Katy Evans, of ants moving flower petals around the body of a dead bee. Within their own colonies, ants will move bodies of deceased ants away from their colonies, so this was interesting. The ring of petals around the bee is both beautiful and unsettling. It also made me think about how interconnected the natural world is, even down to the tiniest of insects.

Acknowledgements …

These poems have been published in the following journals:

"When the bees fly out of your mouth" in *Pinhole Poetry*, Volume 1, Issue 2, in 2022.

"Apian architecture" in the *Consilience* anthology, *Field Notes*, in January 2023.

"Inside Out" was included in a small chapbook titled *Dispatches from the World*, published by the Centre for Creative Writing and Oral Culture at the University of Manitoba. This poem was written in an online Winter 2022 workshop offered by Ariel Gordon.

"In your bones" and "Tiny things" in *The Pi Review*, May 23, 2022. Please note that "In your bones" has been revised for this publication.

"A Note on the Extinction of Brown Bears in Ireland" and "Code" in *Hamilton Arts and Letters*, Fall 2022, 15.2.

"An Elegy for Australia, Burning" in *The Goose*, Volume 18, No. 2, October 2020.

"Once" in *Pinhole Poetry*, Volume 2, Issue 1, April 2023.

"This milkweed's mourning" and "*Discoscapa apicula*" in *The Temz Review* in May 2023.

The poem "In the Bag I Brought Home from Palliative Care on the Night My Mother Died" was shortlisted for *The Fiddlehead*'s 2023 Ralph Gustafson Poetry Contest.

"Cairdeas" in *long con magazine*, Issue 13, in 2023.

… and Thanks to …

For this collection, thanks to Sharon Caseburg, who first heard me read some bee poems online during the pandemic and then heard me say that I thought perhaps they would be part of a section of bee poems in my next book of poetry. She reached out—fairly quickly—and said that she would be interested in reading more of them. Sharon waited a good few years for these bee poems to become a book, and I'm grateful that she could sense their presence as a full-length collection of poems long before I could envision it. She encouraged me along the way, while also being extremely patient. And so many thanks, too, to Jamis Paulson, of Turnstone, for his beautiful book design work.

Thanks especially to Sharon Alkenbrack and Frances Crossan Blanchard, who have understood (and happily encouraged!) my strange fascination with bees. They've nudged me along, even during trying times when the bees were swarming in my life. Thanks, too, to Christine Massimiliano, for her friendship and ongoing encouragement of my writing life. And thanks to those who sat with me in 2022 when everything in my world fell apart all at once—especially Sharon, Frances, Lisa Levecque, Laura-Leigh Gillard, Jessica Watts, and Sarah Gartshore.

Thanks to Laurence Steven and Roger Nash, constant mentors, and ongoing encouragers of my work as a writer since I was in my twenties. Thank you for believing in my work.

To my poetic mentors over the last ten years—Ken Babstock, Yvonne Blomer, John Glenday, Jen Hadfield, and Susan Rich—I've learned so much from you all. Thank you. To Yvonne, especially—so many thanks for introducing me to new poetic forms through your classes at MISSA and online. I'm happily addicted to duplexes, ghazals, long-lined couplets, and triolets now …

Thanks to Lisa O'Connell of Pat the Dog Theatre Creation, along with the City of Greater Sudbury's Arts and Culture Grants, for the microgrant that provided me with time to research the lives of various bee species during the pandemic. Your recognition of my work, and encouragement, is so greatly appreciated.

Thanks to Catherine Banks, for the sanctuary of her Sambro house at Christmas 2022, and for Agatha, my favourite Irish wolfhound. I am so grateful that we are friends…

To Stacy, my sister, who sticks around no matter what. I love you lots.

To Yvonne Blomer, Ariel Gordon, Adrienne Gruber, Tanis MacDonald, and Ken Wilson—thanks for taking such good care of me from so far away over the last few years with your emails, calls, and conversations outside of writing group things.

To the women of The Electronic Garret and The Wild Iris, I'm so grateful for our conversations and shared poems.

To Sarah Ens, whose meticulous copy edits before the final revisions and proofs were brilliant, clear, and wise. Thank you so much for your time and care with my work. I so appreciate it.

Finally, thanks to Alice Major, my editor. I am so deeply grateful that we have had a chance to work together on this project, and I am so thankful for what you have taught me about poetry and revision. I have been a fan of your work for the longest time, and so this has been a joy for me to work with, and learn from, you.